I0842547

Shreibspiegel (The Writing Mirror)

Writing About Writing

Jon Obermeyer

Tomol Press
2018

Copyright ® 2018 Jon Obermeyer and Tomol Press

ISBN: 978-1987527988
First Edition

All rights reserved. No portion of this book may be reproduced in any form without permission from the author, except for brief excerpts for reviews.

"Klutz" and "Stories" appeared in *Briarcliff: A Memoir of 1985-1993*.

"Density" originally appeared in *The Harbor: The Innocence Before 9/11*.

"Learning to Surf" originally appeared in different format in *Myriad*.

Cover photo by author: *Still Life with Writing Desk*

To my writing teachers and emergency room doctors

Also by Jon Obermeyer

The Reassurance of Ghosts (poems)

The Winter Practice (short stories)

The Low Wire: Meditations on Loss and Creative
Restoration (essays)

It Happens That Fast: A Santa Barbara Memoir

Salispuedes (poems)

Centripetal Force (short stories)

Briarcliff: 1985-1993 (memoir)

The Harbor: 1993-2001 (memoir)

The Guests (memoir)

Occupational Hazards (poems)

Myriad: A Poet's Guide to the Writing Life

Analog: Creativing Relevance Trust and Loyalty in a
Digital World (with Mike Lingo and John Miller)

Contents

Introduction

About the Author

The limit of my language is the limit of my world
- Ludwig Wittgenstein

There is nothing to writing. Just sit down at a typewriter and bleed.
— Ernest Hemingway

The pleasure of writing is like eating a big juicy steak with loose teeth.
- Roy Blount, Jr.

Schreibspeigel
(The Writing Mirror)

Introduction

We write to taste life twice.
- Anais Nin

Accidents, mistakes and gaffes move us forward.

In 1946, Raytheon engineer Percy Spencer tested a military-grade magnetron in the lab and realized the chocolate snack in his pocket had melted. While trying to improve the power level of the magnetron tubes used in radar sets, Spencer accidentally invented the "radar-range" or as we like to call it, the microwave oven.

Like Spencer's melted candy bar, the best writing is accidental, or a result of playing around or distraction. Just ask the three princes from the island of Serendip (located near Sri Lanka) who were always stumbling into new adventures.

Maurice Sendak's *Where The Wild Things Are* was originally titled Where The Wild Horses Are, but Sendak couldn't draw horses, only "things." So, there you go.

Samuel Richardson owned a printing press. To test its capabilities he wrote sample letters for an etiquette manual, including didactic letters to help servant girls deal with lecherous employers. He eventually developed his pamphlet into something called *Pamela*, a bestseller that is now considered the first modern English novel.

Atlanta author Margaret "Peggy" Mitchell twisted her ankle. She couldn't leave the house. She asked her husband to go to the library often to pick up more books for her. Exasperated at having to haul the heavy hardbacks home, Mitchell's husband joked, "For God's sake, Peggy, can't you write a book instead of reading them?"

John Fowles had another novel in the works the day he spotted the enigmatic woman in the dark cape staring out to sea from the quay in Dorset. His literary detour became the greater-known The French Lieutenant's Woman. (I don't know what happened to the book he abandoned).

In early 2018, Brooks Roddan had asked me to submit writing-themed blogs for his IF SF Publishing website. He published two blogs. I lobbed in two more and had two more in the queue waiting for him.

If six eggs make a delicious and filling Denver omelet, and six showgirls make for a memorable weekend, then six blogs is critical mass for something.

That's when book flashed onto my brain like the garish neon outside Caesar's Palace. I heard the Universe give a hearty chuckle and my Muse gave me her usual "you are such a dweeb!" look.

So then, damen und herren a writing book about writing.

I had to find a title. I thought surely the Germans have a precise term for this like freudenschade and festschrift and zeitgeist. Hence, schreibspiegel, the mirror held up to writing. Over-the-top clever, in my mind. And for the first time in my 59 years, the name of Spiegel catalogue made sense.

The other thing about using German terms Is that they drive the Spell Check software feature crazy, underlined words in red everywhere!

I began populating the manuscript with my blogs, riffs, tall tales and random musings about writing.

I collect and post writer quotes, and sometimes I write a blog using the writer quote as the prompt.

My 2017-eclipse-inspired writing guide Myriad covered 48
writing topics, most of them standard fare (feature writing,
travel writing, poetry, fiction, self-publishing). This mirror book
would be an illogical omnibus representing a plate of reheated
leftovers (in a microwave of course), the deleted scenes
feature from a movie and a gaggle of red-haired stepchildren.

Entrepreneurs talk about a launching a new company as the
dual act of building an airplane and flying an airplane, and
how you can't do both at once. This book pulls it off, I think.

Bethesda, NC
May, 2018

Motivation

*We write books because our children are not interested in us.
We address ourselves to an anonymous world because our
wives plug their ears when we speak to them.*
     -   Milan Kundera

I don't know where this thing came from.

I'm an author. My children, to my knowledge, are not writers.
My mother is a composer of Christian hymns, but not an
author of my books. My father was an accountant, and late in
life, a driver of Enduro races and a volunteer park ranger.

Perhaps writing skips a generation. My grandfather Grey, a
grocer, wrote Ogden Nash-style poems on special occasions
like my birthday. Maybe my daughters will have children one
day, and those offspring will pick up the pen.

Writing chose me, but there was never an official coronation,
an onboarding, an orientation, or a launch event. There was
no Road to Damascus or Belly of the Whale conversion. The
author thing formed, like a sandbar from river sediment, over
time.

I'm home sick in 4th grade. I sneak an index card into my
bedroom and write down a simple stanza, a pair of couplets
about Christopher Columbus. I am proud of the rhyme
scheme: knowing/showing, New World/unfurled.

I go for a six-mile run my senior year in high school, from
our house in the Montecito foothills to the ocean at East
Beach. It's a rainy, Sunday afternoon. I write down everything
I observe and hear along the way in a stream-of-conscious
style. The poem is published in my high school literary
magazine.

We read John Updike's short story "A&P" on a warm autumn afternoon in Montecito. The windows in the classroom are open. The prevailing westerly breeze rustles the leaves in the eucalyptus. We can hear the tennis team practicing on nearby courts, the plock-pause-plock, plock-pause-plock of steady forehand returns, an echo of Updike's musical supermarket cash register. I decide that want to write a story like that someday.

A year later, I'm taking an early morning hike on a low peak above Edinburgh, Scotland. I'd been observing spectacular sunrises for 20 years along the Southern California coast. This sunrise is different. The city below me is 850 years old. I like the way Firth of Forth sounds. My parents have just divorced. I've been seeing four plays a day at the Festival and drinking Carlsberg Elephant lager, and I still have jet lag. The rain clouds remind me of a blanket. Something clicks.

I may not ever make more than $300 a year in Amazon royalties. I don't care about fame; it will be less than two minutes. Maybe the best I can hope for is to be able to read one poem at the monthly open mic night at Flyleaf Books in Chapel Hill.

There might never be accolades or agents. There might only be this perpetual impulse, to populate a blank page with what interests me that day, what I can render elegantly by sundown.

To quote Auden on the death of Yeats, on Yeats' gift for writing poetry: "It survives, a way of happening, a mouth."

The Well

Talent doesn't write one page; it writes 300 pages…The strong do not hesitate. They exhaust ink. They use up paper. In Literature, there are only oxen.
—Jules Renard

I have 16 books I want to write.

As soon as I finish one book, I move on to the next book (the same weekend), like a chain smoker, lighting one manuscript off the dying embers of the previous one.

Over the winter, I hibernated and worked on a memoir of my late 20's and early 30's, and dedicated it to my eldest daughter, who was born during that interesting epoch of Reagan-Bush (senior).

My youngest daughter (born in Clinton's first term) asked indignantly, "where's my book?"

So last evening, I outlined her book, spanning the first Twin Tower bombing (Feb 26,1993), up to the real thing on 9/11. I want Liz' book to be about the innocence prior to 9/11, our suburban family story mirroring a naive nation.

The Twin Towers collapsed immediately and our family unit disbanded about 20 months later. But we rebounded and regrouped quite nicely.

I want this new book to talk about the upside, how this unexpected upheaval allowed those of us who were open to it (or devastated by it indirectly) to restore personal authenticity and soul.

It will be fun book, and I'm 2,500 words into it.

Yesterday I topped out a client's business book at 110 pages. We might push it in final draft form to 120 pages or 150 pages. And then he has another book behind it he wants me to help him write.

This morning I am writing this chapter. This afternoon I will be writing a client's blog on food safety in fast food dining, and website copy for a tech company. I may even write a poem before the weekend is over.

I think back to a fallow period, from 1996 to 2004, when I hardly wrote anything. I was busy raising a family, aerating and mowing a suburban Greensboro lawn, coaching youth soccer, working on my career, managing and then buying a convention services business (100-hour workweeks, supporting events throughout the Southeast U.S.).

I am about to turn 60. I'm an empty nester who works from home. I write every day. It's like a well I can keep coming back to for water; it never dries up.

What is that you do? People will ask me.

I will tell them I am an ox.

Double-Take

It's all about paying attention. Attention is vitality. It connects you with others. It makes you eager. Stay eager.
-Susan Sontag

Mom said look both ways when crossing the street. It seemed silly at the time.

I should thank her more often.

Looking left I see a garbage truck barreling along in my direction (seeking barrels). The men were out on strike that year and I wondered if these guys passing in front of me were the other-worldly creatures known as scabs.

Looking right I see a station wagon with wood paneling slowing for me. The driver could have been part of a diamond heist. He is wearing a suit with a necktie. He is dressed to make loans at the bank. There are bags of groceries in the way-back. Men don't usually drive a car like that.

Two glances, ten seconds, two different worlds.

Fifty years later, I adhere to my mom's guidance.

I am a fan of redundancy, a perfected double-look to scan and flank the whole field of battle.

It earns you twice the creative source material and it's the safest path to crossing the street, toward Insight and Compassion.

The Poet and the Whole Enchilada

The poet walks the earth in relative obscurity. You might see him surface briefly at an open mic. poetry event or at a fiction workshop in a hotel ballroom, but for the most part he stays in his burrow.

The poet has made $300 lifetime directly from poetry, the result of a prize from his undergraduate days, sponsored by a woman's literary club in Montecito. The poetry journals used to pay him in printed copies (no more than two copies). Now they pay nothing at all, and charge reading fees.

So, the poet keeps his day job. The poet's bosses loves him. He can sum up a one-hour staff meeting in three words. He'll write up something funny for the Christmas holiday party, a nativity pageant mimicking the best lines of The Love Song of J. Alfred Prufrock.

The poet writes elegant copy and sticks to his knitting. You hardly know he's there in his cubicle.

His wife and his kids worry about him. His doctor would like to see him walking more often, hills especially.

He's happiest on a rainy, Saturday morning, when the traffic is lighter on the road, and only a few of his neighbors are stirring. He doesn't like the sound of a leaf blower or someone repairing a dirt bike in the driveway, though he's fine with your lawnmower and band saw (apropos of Studs Terkel, Phil Levine and Walt Whitman)

The poet is happiest with the simplest of things: sourdough toast and apricot jam, an etymology dictionary, or a 700-age biography of Josef Stalin (also a poet, in his younger pre-purge days).

He is interested and amused by just about anything lying around: last month's light bill (especially the four-color chart explaining hot water usage), the Viet-Thai menu at lunch (including typos) at lunch, or a dated airplane boarding pass (SJC to EWR). His ADD serves him well.

The poet is an introvert, but not really.

He reaches out boldly to every particulate on the planet, because everything is *subject* to him (he delights in this double meaning).

The entire enchilada is fair game: Ebola ambulance drivers, Tottenham Hotspur hooligans at a Premiere League football match, Polish refugees, linotype operators, panhandlers, rookie pitchers at spring training, theoretical physicists, circus aerialists, pile driver operators and West Marin ecologists.

The poet is billionaire and bugler, vogler and ogler, voyeur and king.

He is a generalist who specializes to the nth degree.

Today he might choose to write about just about anything.

Ending Writers Block in Our Lifetime.

Eventually, science finds a cure: polio, smallpox, measles, whooping cough, rinderpest (look it up); all gone.

Eventually, those ladies and gents in the white lab coats wielding pipettes will get around to the debilitating condition known as Writer's Block.

Imagine if Big Pharma spent $1 Billion and 14 years of R&D effort on Writers Block, just like they do on allergy medicine and mood lifters. The commercial might sound like this:

"Ask your doctor if **Narrativa** is right for you. Narrativa is a fast-flow, editor-inhibitor (FFEI) that works in your bloodstream to initiate poetry, prose and young adult fiction. Side effects of Narrativa include job loss, missed meals, laptop battery wear, comma splices, and of course, death. For impoverished literary journal writers and creative writing program faculty adjuncts, Pfizer may be willing to subsidize the cost of your Narrativa dosing."

Maybe it's my undiagnosed, adult-onset ADD, but I rarely have a problem with writer's block, a daunting blank page, or picking a topic.

I read a lot and that helps.

I was recently reading a small Joan Didion book "South and West: From a Notebook" (2017), and she had a line in there about the prevalence of mattresses secured to car rooftops in the Mississippi in the 1970's.

So, I immediately created a blank Word doc and wrote "Mattresses" as the title and saved it. I'll come back to it later to riff on the initial visual, and credit Didion of course.

One Saturday evening, I was reading a profile of an eighty year old female playwright in The New Yorker, and I looked at the photograph and thought, "this could be my mother."

I immediately started a short story with the premise that my mother broke off her engagement with my dad in 1957 (which meant she didn't conceive me in 1958), and pursued her talent as a pianist and arranger for gospel quartets. In my story, her prescient career move, her talent and her perfect pitch, will land her in the middle of 1960's folk-rock music scene in Los Angeles, where she will link up with a fictional version of Michael Omartian, a Christian music producer famous for his work with those heathens, Steely Dan.

With this storyline, I now have a second story.

What happened to my father after that break-up? How would his life turn out? And then, with genius and care, I will bring my not-mom and my not-dad back together at their 50th college reunion in 2007 in Santa Barbara (my parents divorced in 1978 and actually did go to their college reunion together).

The next morning, while eating an Everything bagel, I was back in The New Yorker, trolling. I read a piece by the art critic Peter Schjeldahl about the opening of an exhibit by the Spanish painter Francisco de Zurbaran about the biblical "Jacob and His Twelve Sons" (1640–45), the dozen offspring who became the twelve tribes of Israel. I have two adult daughters; what the hell would it be like to raise twelve sons?

I brought the Jacob story fast-forward from the Book of Genesis to the present day. I imagine Jacob's front yard strewn with the detritus of Big Wheels, Schwinn Stingrays and Triumph 500cc motorcycles. I make him a grocer because going to the grocery store for 18 people (the total household) every week became burndensome for both wives ("90 minutes just in the check-out line."), so they just built their own family Piggly-Wiggly location in back of the house.

So much for this flood-tide of material, most of it based on tiny prompts and snippets I read about or overhear.

Is what I produce prolifically any good? The jury is still out. I happen to think the quality is as high as ever; I'm just undiscovered, right?

What I do know is that I have a clipboard next to my writing desk, with a handwritten list of sixteen potential writing projects, poems, stories, plays, books that I'd like to tackle, and I'm sure I will, eventually. The one problem I don't have is writer's block.

Altered States

"I've seen the U.S. from the bottom up."
-   Junot Diaz

I.
In my almost sixty years, I have lived in three states.

I was born and raised in Southern California and I've lived
in North Carolina for almost three decades. I made a slight
detour to West Florida in my early fifties and had an apartment
near the Gulf of Mexico, unfortunately without a dock out back
or a proper fishing skiff.

I have visited most every state, except for Hawaii, Alaska and
both Dakotas. Oklahoma, Nebraska and Iowa have eluded me
so far, and I'm sure they have their reasons. In my estimate,
six more states to go. I'm not sure what it is that will take me
to Tulsa or Omaha or Ames, but I used to say the same thing
about Wichita.

II.
As a young child, my grandmother Dorothy (a widow) took me
with her on the train and on Greyhound to most of the western
states, on trips to the Grand Canyon, Yellowstone, Mt. Rainier
and Victoria in British Columbia.

My parents took me out of school each spring to ski in Aspen
and Vail, a 19-hour drive through Nevada, Utah and western
Colorado to get there. There's a hundred mile stretch of
eastern Utah with absolutely nothing, between Salina and
Green River. There's a truck stop in Beaver, Utah with t-bone
steaks as wide as a small pizza.

When my parents divorced in 1978, my college breaks found
me shuttling between Colorado and Washington. My dad
retired to Tucson. I got custody of Arizona at the end of his life.

I've been fortunate to have friends from college who have settled in different parts of the country, including the Midwest, New England and the Deep South.

A visit to southern New Hampshire means day trips to the Maine coast and into Boston. A visit to Mississippi expands west to include New Orleans. When I went to Rockford, Illinois to see Pat, that usually meant a Cubs game at Wrigley and a Snappers minor league game up in Beloit, across the line in Wisconsin.

III.
My work used to take me around the country.

As an economic developer, I filled in for a colleague on a recruiting trip to Chicago. I started my morning on Lake Street near the United Center and housing projects, calling on a kosher gefilte fish processor with barbed wire atop the parking lot fence. By mid-day I was in suburban Naperville, meeting with an agricultural products firm. I finished my day in the Loop in an office tower meeting with a Fortune 500 printing conglomerate. By seven p.m., I was on a flight home to North Carolina.

I used to own a convention services business, which meant 180 events per year in eight states, including Pennsylvania for a log home show. I've worked in hundreds of hotels and convention centers, but I would not recognize the front entrance of any of them. Our line of work meant we backed our trucks up to the loading docks, and often pushed our equipment past the kitchen or housekeeping department.

I attended a trade show conference in northern Illinois, at a beautiful resort near Lake Geneva. On the last day, I bailed on the seminars and drove to Delavan, the original home of the Ringling Brothers circus. I then drove over to Madison, then all the way up Wisconsin to Green Bay to see Lambeau

Field, followed by a drive home along the western shore of Lake Michigan at sunset. I stopped several times at scenic overlooks and once went down to onto the beach to collect smooth stones.

I was reminded of the *Nick Adams Stories* by Hemingway, which are set along the shores of the same lake, much further north.

A venture capital conference took me out to Little Rock and up to Rochester, where I planned a side trip to Cooperstown and my grandfather's birthplace in Hudson.

A few years ago, the software start-up I worked for moved its operations from Sausalito to Wichita, Kansas, in order to save on labor costs and slow down the "burn rate" on the venture capital from investors. The CEO, a Wichita native, asked me to work there two weeks each month, and then asked me to move there. I turned him down.

Wichita had super cheap rent and surprisingly good sushi. I liked the funky little village of Delano, as well as the inspiring Keeper of the Plains, a 44-foot-high steel sculpture by the Kiowa-Comanche artist Blackbear Bosin that stands guard at the confluence of the Arkansas and Little Arkansas rivers.

I just couldn't see myself living there, so far from any ocean. Although I once had someone tell me if you get out onto the plains, walking through the prairie grass feels like wading in shallow water at edge of a giant sea, which was how it was there in the Jayhawk State millions of years ago.

IV.
Wanderlust has helped me as a writer. It's a way of filling the tank with subject matter for poems, short stories and creative non-fiction.

I remember going to a summer evening rehearsal of
the Mormon Tabernacle Choir in Salt Lake City with my
grandmother as a ten-year-old.

At age fifteen, my mom took me to see Impressionist paintings
at the Art Institute of Chicago. Following college graduation, I
drove a friend's car from Santa Barbara to Chicago, stopping
over in Kansas City and Hannibal, Missouri on the way.

I've been in New Orleans, during the silent and sober week
following Mardi Gras. I was in Austin, Texas the weekend
before 9/11.

Tonight, I was thinking of the five years in a row that I made
it my goal to spend 30 days each year in Florida, mostly in
Jacksonville beaches and in St. Petersburg.

I'm thinking of all the house concerts, open mics and local
music festivals I've been to in Atlantic Beach, Florida, and that
wonderful early spring day in 2017 driving all over Nassau
County, Florida with my friend Matt Soergel, chasing down
a feature story about Peter Hooper, an early 20th Century
African-American magician known as the "Second Houdini."

I still remember the crude wooden pews and framing in the
doorway in that country church in Nassauville where Hooper's
nephew showed us the scrapbook clippings of his famous
uncle.

Many people have been to Nassau County, Florida. They
just didn't know it. They breezed through it on Interstate
95 on their way to or from Orlando and Key West. They
probably remember exit 373 (Yulee), fifteen miles south of the
Georgia border, your last chance to buy Florida citrus in large
quantities.

V.

I'm fairly sedentary these days. I work from home. I might walk
to the mailbox or visit a nearby hiking trail on the Eno River.
I teach writing workshops 45 minutes away at a community
college in the rural North Carolina town of Pittsboro.
Downtown Pittsboro might remind you of Mayberry. The 19th
county courthouse is the central point in town, and the state
highway makes a loop so you can go around it.

I travel to San Francisco four to five times a year for work.
I've expanded my Bay Area trips to include Sacramento,
specifically Fair Oaks and Folsom (like the prison and the
Johnny Cash song). I spent a summer in nearby Chico during
high school, working the peach, plum and almond harvest,
bailing hay and cleaning calf pens.

I also visit family in Ventura, north of Los Angeles. When
possible, I head up the coast highway to my hometown of
Santa Barbara, recently devastated by fires and mudslides.

My best friend John and his wife recently moved from Marin
County to Santa Fe, and I'm looking forward to visiting there.

They're building a house in Galisteo, a bend in the road
north of town with spectacular views, and at last count, 253
residents. Burl Ives used to live there. They film westerns
there, movies like The Cowboys, Silverado and Young Guns.
The area is rich in taqueria, rusted, antique Chevrolet pick-up
trucks, and perhaps a few fiber-art studios.

New Mexico is called Land of Enchantment for a reason. I'm
sure a poem or a story will come out of it.

The Watchmaker

*As the evening breeze begins to blow over the darkening hills
of the desert, you pick up your pen and start writing again,
working like an old-fashioned watchmaker, with a magnifying
glass in your eye and a pair of tweezers between your fingers.*
-Amos Oz

I.
Driving along the outer beltline in Raleigh the other day, I
passed a small utility van with promotional writing on the side
announcing that the driver (or a passenger) was a "Grout
Doctor." I wondered what that meant; a proficiency in cleaning,
removing or installing grout, or a holy trinity of all three?
Does it take an advanced degree and a two-year residency,
or undergraduate courses in biology and organic chemistry?
Does a caulk gun require a conceal-and-carry permit?

The next day in historic Beaufort, my friend Craig pointed out
where the sidewalk had buckled but some human being had
shaved down the buckled end to an amazing smoothness,
a flat surface so I wouldn't trip. Who are these Sidewalk
Shavers, we wondered? What implement would they wield
and when do the sidewalk czars in public works determine an
aberration requires such intensive surgery?

Later that morning, I met a woman at the Beaufort farmers
market who is an official "reef maker." Her company takes
hulks of decommissioned seagoing vessels and sinks them
into the deep off Cape Lookout to create artificial reefs. She
told me it's an elaborate two-year process of government
permitting to gut a ship of all accouterment and equipment to
make it "reef worthy." There's also an art to the final sinking,
so you don't capsize the vessel that towed the reef out to sea.
The company was selling raffle tickets to observe the next
sinking, a retired ferry boat, they would deep-six off Cape
Hatteras.

II.
Grout Doctor, Sidewalk Shaver, Reef Maker: these are just
three professions of many that you've probably never heard
off. John McPhee might give you a full book on each one,
where I only provided a paragraph.

I am fascinated by occupations.

Most writers have a standard bartender-barge tender-busboy
resume, for street cred., I guess so you know you can trust
them (and their scar tissue and callouses).

Kerouac set the bar high for literary stintsmanship (cotton
picker, dishwasher, gas station attendant, deckhand and
railroad brakeman).

Faulkner worked as a night watchman in a power plant.
William S. Burroughs was a bug exterminator and Saul Bellow
was a social worker.

Arthur Conan Doyle was a ship's surgeon. Agatha Christie
and I both worked as pharmacy assistants, though mine was
not a battlefield assignment.

The best-selling novelist of 2023 will probably claim she
"started out as an Uber driver and telemarketer."

III.

I don't know if Amos Oz ever worked as a watchmaker or a
watchmaker's assistant, but occupations do provide writers
with endless sources of material, including analogies to the
writing craft.

This is why I have always enjoyed the poetry of the late Phil
Levine, often set in raw settings like ball bearing factories
or the assembly line at Ford's River Rouge plant in Detroit.

My first job in high school was auction runner. I also worked
afternoons after class at the Castagnola Brother's seafood
market, where I helped unload swordfish and made the clam
chowder each Tuesday for the Lobster House chain (think
Red Lobster, before Red Lobster).

That job showed up in my first college short story (a direct
rip-off/homage to John Updike's "A&P") and in a lovely poem
called "Identity." Here are the final nine lines:

> I wore a too-thin smock
> over my school clothes,
> and I punched-in each
> afternoon as if I was about
> to lose fingers. You try it.
>
> To the rest of them there,
> I was but a dabbler: defined
> by the day's inky time-stamp,
> the beginning of an afterthought.

IV.
Melville was a bank clerk in Albany and George Orwell was a
cop in Burma. I never was in law enforcement, but do have 15
years in the banking field.

My first job out of college (after working as a temp. in store
inventory at Macy's) was bank teller in southwest San
Francisco. No literary connection there, though I wrote bad,
un-publishable poems in my time off. A year later, I moved
back to hometown of Santa Barbara and found a position as
a vault teller in a catacomb underneath the main branch. We
processed the school system cafeteria bags:

> The wadded ones and fives, the damp checks
> Reeking of steamed meat and carrots,
> Fruit cups and cookies

As the collection point for seven branches, we usually had a million dollars a day or more moving through our vault, and this stream of currency captivated my imagination:

> Twenties, tens, fives and ones,
> the sweat of a hundred thousand palms
> and a million fingers, curing moist
> between the bills. Moisture of commerce,
> crucial as evaporation and downpour rain.
>
> Every day at four, we send our city south
> by armored car. Nameless citizens of coin,
> crowds of currency that pass silently
> from hand to hand, never enough to save.

I later morphed my poem "Vault Teller" into a short story, a sardonic tale of bundled currency, embezzlement and machismo:

To complete the management trainee program at the Carrillo Bank & Trust, you had to successfully repossess a vehicle on your own.

Senior management deemed repossession as the ideal rite of passage. All those accounting and marketing courses in college, were for naught, as well as the months of classroom training and rotations in mortgage lending, loan servicing, commercial loans and teller line duty. If you can't repossess then you have no business making a loan or running a branch.

I also had fun rendering the my underling interactions with the bank's management:

Rod Chavez ran the main branch with an unstated closed-door policy. Handle it, was his motto. He probably had that mantra tattooed on one of his arms, alongside the Semper Fi.

Handle it, says it all. If you're in a firefight in a jungle, I
guess you want Chavez beside you, but here in peacetime,
it's better for everyone if he remains undisturbed in his glass
corner office, reading print-outs and writing up reports.

*I saw him relax once at the company picnic held in a
county park. He walked up and spoke to me on his way to
throw horseshoes. I'd worked for him for a year, at that point.*

Is your wife here today?

I'm not married, I reminded him.

V.
Let's return to Amos Oz' watchmaker.

What he is mostly about with this metaphor is the precision
and care that a writer brings to his or her craft.

Here's the rest of the watchmaker quote:

*…holding and inspecting an adjective against the light,
changing a faulty adverb, tightening a loose verb, reshaping a
worn-out idiom.*

What I'm really picking up on here with the Oz analogy is
Writer as auto mechanic.

I recently had my VW in the shop for repairs. I'd hit a large
piece of tractor-trailer tire retread at about 68 m.p.h. and it had
done a good bit of damage to my radiator.

My mechanic George and his assistants had taken apart the
entire front-end of my car in order to replace the radiator, and
along the way had replaced cracked valves and hoses.

Sometimes a story or a poem needs more than a tune-up,
an oil change or Turtle Wax rubbed with a chamois cloth.

Sometimes you have to put your story in the shop, put it up on the lift and get underneath it. Or you need a rebuilt engine.

In this way of thinking, the writer is clad in coveralls and inhabits dank caverns and pits, removed from sunlight. The phrase grease monkey comes to mind. He knows his way around alternators, timing belts, coolants, pistons and brake lines. There is nothing refined or elegant about it.

Guitar Players

"Know your own bone" – Thoreau

in "The Writing Life" (1989), Annie Dillard advises us to "Write
as if you were dying…write for an audience consisting solely
of terminal patients. What would you begin writing if you knew
you would die soon? What could you say to a dying person
that would not enrage by its triviality?

The irony of Dillard's advice is you have to write about trivial
things (coffee pots, foot corns, squirrels, laundry hampers)
in order to expand upon objects and make a more poignant,
universal statement. You can't start by writing about Life,
Death, Love or Grief. You have to back your way into it using a
concrete image as your starting point.

Pay attention to serendipity, to the accidental drop-shipment of
material right into you lap

One evening in Southern Pines, NC, I was invited at the last
minute to observe a musical jam session: nine senior-age
men seated in a circle playing guitar, mandolin and fiddle,
passing a baton of song (covers and originals) among each
other.

The session was not performance hall quality, but very high on
charm and entertainment, and joy. I felt like I was watching a
documentary film. I wrote a poem about it the next day and I
can see the possibility of a short story or a novel growing out
of that evening.

While I watched them play, I thought about the life wisdom it
takes to sing a ballad earnestly, and the experience playing
music to know the possible chord variations when the key
is announced, so you can follow along without necessarily
knowing a song. Music is a metaphor for many things.

Eat a Peach

Pick a summer, any summer. Go back in time and pluck that ripe peach of a memory. Bring it back to us in all its glory, and regale us with details. Is it a Freestone or a Cling peach? Is it green and hard from too early picking or is it fiery and fuzzy in its ripeness?

Don't just tell us about moonlit walks along an ocean boardwalk or through a tobacco field. Tell us what it sounded like, and what it tasted like. Take the ordinary, expected rendering and stand it on its head.

If you're going to summon a cicada, it should be a cicada like I've never heard it described. The same goes for kudzu, and

Hold off on the import of the memory. That might take some discipline. Load your first summer memory with as much scrumptious detail as possible and let the words carry the weight. Let your language distill the memory, from the Latin distillare to trickle down in minute drops.

And here's the weird balancing act. You want to render that summary memory with both poignancy (literally, with a sharp point to it), and subtlety (fine, thin, delicate, subject to dissolving).

Okay, pick a point forward in time (it doesn't have to be summer). How did the events of that summer transform you (or others), how did they remembered moments redeem (or possibly destroy) your future sense of self?

I picked the summer of 1974, a summer when my parents shipped me off to my aunt's farm in the Sacramento Valley to pick peaches, plums and almonds. In early August, Nixon resigned the presidency and a week later I turned sixteen.

My parents' intent was to straighten me out with hard labor,
but what I really suspect is that it was a dry run for me being
out of the house. Three years later they abruptly moved to
Colorado and four years later divorced. My "farm summer"
was a test bed for my parents to temporarily empty the nest
and see what it felt like. It was a separation they intuitively
instigated. They did it for their own good.

Writer in Residence

I.
The one-week residency is housed in a restored mansion in the middle of North Carolina, an hour's drive from Raleigh.

The drive is easy, all four-lane highway, with a minimum of traffic lights and gravel trucks to be stuck behind.

The adjacent town is quaint, with a toy-like train station, art galleries, wine bars, cafes and coffee shops. It's like a Blowing Rock or Beaufort translated to the Sandhills region of the Piedmont. The surrounding area is known for its golf and horseback riding, a picturesque retirement and resort area symbolized by the pinecone.

Settled by Scots, the houses have an English country village feel to them, like the setting of a popular BBC murder mystery featuring bumbling but clever detectives.

Many of the local cottages sell for a million dollars or more. There are 600 realtors in a county of 88,000 residents, which should tell you something.

The residency house was built in the 1920s and is on the National Register of Historic Places. It is Colonial Revival style, a two-story brick main house plus "rambling" additions.

There is literary inspiration everywhere. The mansion's original owner was a novelist and newspaper publisher. He had three separate libraries: reference works, dictionaries, and favorite authors. A large room in the upper wing houses the North Carolina Literary Hall of Fame. F. Scott Fitzgerald was over-served during a stay here in 1935 and got into a literary feud with his Southern hosts.

There's a circular gravel drive out front, with horses grazing nearby. I decide I will write a poem about the horses, or gravel.

II.
The recommended residency is one week, from Monday afternoon to the next Monday morning. Some writers stay two weeks in a row, which would definitely be too much solitude and buffer for me to bear.

An arts non-profit runs the place. There is an executive director who arranges writer selection, and a caretaker who helps me settle me in. There is no charge for the lodging, but a small donation is encouraged upon departure.

The Writers quarters are upstairs at the back of the house. For all the reverence given to resident writers, the official entrance is next to the downstairs catering kitchen. You're here to write novels and finish manuscripts, but you're still the help.

There are four single bedrooms with literary names: Thomas Wolf (the largest), Maxwell Perkins, Sherwood Anderson and Paul Green. There are sitting rooms and small hallway libraries, common areas with reading chairs and obscure books. Each room contains a single bed, a tasteful period bureau, framed artwork, a sitting chair and a desk. Some rooms have a splendid view of the gardens; others face the parking area. Forget the view. You are here to write.

III.
Isolation is encouraged, and a library-like quiet is enforced.

Socialization occurs in the kitchen, around the coffee bean grinder and the stove with the tea kettle. Two writers chit chat one morning and return to their respective book projects: one is writing experimental short stories, the other a monograph on Canadian female documentary filmmakers.

Around 2 p.m. one afternoon, the fourth writer emerges in her bathrobe and makes her way to the kitchen, for a cold lunch (breakfast?) of spicy chicken and Brussels sprouts, eaten directly out of Tupperware containers she has brought from home. She lives in Durham, but is originally from Nigeria.

Her African/English is a bit difficult for me to understand, yet I must also admit I had trouble understanding North Carolinians when I first moved here from California thirty years ago.

With almost 200 million residents, I had no idea that Nigeria was the biggest country in Africa by population and the seventh most populous country in the world. There are over 500 ethnic groups in Nigeria, and this writer is part of the Yoruba group, one of the largest. She is writing a nonfiction book about toxic families, based on a popular newspaper column for a Lagos paper she had written earlier in the year.

IV.
It's a competitive process to earn a residency, but from my observation highly collegial once you're here.

Most of us live in communities and cultures where writing is not highly valued (unless you area famous writer).

Most of us grind away in relative obscurity (publishing in literary journals that only pay in copies). Most of us have day jobs as teachers, freelance writers or waiters, to pay the bills.

So, it's a relief to huddle briefly under one roof with other writers. There's a common base of understanding: we all know what a rejection slip looks like, and we have a small loyal following among family and friends, who may or may not read what we write and publish. They are mostly in awe of us that we have kept at it over the years, paid mostly in the satisfaction of the work itself.

It's a luxury to have an entire week just to write, no schedule and no interruptions other than the ones I'm willing to invent.

It can be intimidating to have this much seclusion. It reminds me of the time I participated in a 24-hour "solo" in a redwood forest outside Santa Cruz, with nothing but my sleeping bag, my bible and a container of drinking water. It was a group activity organized by a bible camp. I was placed in a clearing, with my closest peer about 100 yards away; in my line of sight but too far away for conversation.

I was seventeen years old. It was way too much solitude and I was glad when it was over. I barely read the bible. I mostly stared up at the redwoods and waited for nightfall or the whole thing to be over.

The first full day of residency, I read a novel, wrote two poems and took two naps. Now, on my second day, I'm starting to get the hang of it, the flow and the momentum to tackle a much larger project.

I think I will take a walk later. I'm going to go talk to the horses.

Meant to Mentor

Sometimes we start with a gift, without the prospect of compensation or fees. It's what we do as writers, who thrive in a community of writers. I recently met a young writer, in his mid 20's, and for two afternoons we sat in a quiet room of a writer's residency house and "workshopped" two of his poems: he shared his poem in digital form, then read it aloud, and then I gave him notes, which he used to refine his poem there on the spot.

First, we cut the fluff. By reading a poem aloud to another human, the poet can often hear for the first time a clunky, cumbersome or confusing line. I told him: "If you run out breath reading your line, that means it's too long. Break it up into two, or even three sentences, and that will punch it up."

We also looked at individual words, probing for weakness. I believe a poem is more powerful when you build a cadence of single-syllable words, which are made up of hard consonants, especially at the line break. This poet had many gerunds at the end of his lines, and when he reverted to the original verb, or moved the weaker "ing" sound to a less prominent position, it made the poems more powerful.

I used a Socratic approach to my critique: "What did you mean when you picked this title?" "What is this line meant to accomplish?"

It was mostly an exercise in pruning. We cut each poem by 15-20%, and I didn't ask him to change much of what he'd already written. Too often editors ask writers to make something the way they would do it, and don't let pieces evolve organic to their own strengths.

I shared several of my poems, and was open to his critique. I wanted to show how a lifelong poet keeps on producing new work. This young man has 40 years of writing ahead of him.

The Unexpected Fan: A Meditation on Fame

You and B. went to college together, a small liberal arts school in Southern California, so tiny that you saw everyone else at least twice a day.

You haven't seen B. in 35 years.

B. invites you to visit next time you are in the Bay Area.

B. is a gracious host.

You meet his teenage daughter. When she hears your name she smiles and says, "oh, the author." It's a moment of pure dopamine. You want to cry.

B.'s brother is a writer and a voiceover artist. That probably helps.

B drives a big ass pick-up truck and has a ski boat in the driveway. He is a redneck who makes fun of other rednecks and doesn't mind the irony of it.

B. recently discovered a one-ton slab of granite buried in his front yard. He wrangled it to the surface so it stands upright like a monolith from the movie 2001. He threw his back out but doesn't seem to mind.

B. takes you out to breakfast at his favorite spot, the Country Kitchen, and tells you don't hold back, order the steak and eggs. He picks up the check and takes the side biscuit home for his wife.

At breakfast, B. reminds you that another friend, M., dragged him out to your senior poetry reading back in the fall of 1979, the same time as the hostages in Iran. He remembers you read your England poems and on a boom box you played a cassette of Pat Metheny to set the mood for the evening.

You recall a poem about the train leaving London, and you compared it to a glowworm in a garden, he reminds you. You are astonished. That poem does not exist anywhere, except in B.'s memory, and maybe a few other classmates who were there in Reynold's Hall that night.

B. buys a copies of all your books, as they are published. They are all out on his home office desk, ready for you to sign them.

You nickname him "Tote Bag." It's a fundraiser and among all your friends and patrons, he has spent at the highest level.

It's fair to say after four decades of writing, you don't have much of a following. You write quietly and for the most part unrecognized in a precious bubble of obscurity.

But among your friends and family, there's not another fan of your work like B. that you can think of.

Three Paragraphs Outside Durham, North Carolina

I.   Baking
I don't revise my poems, other than tweaking a word or two.
They plop onto the page, intact, like a cake whose center
doesn't collapse due to too much moisture (it helps if you
use that high-fat European butter). I spend most of my time
accumulating and shelving ingredients. Somewhere in my
cerebral cortex there must be a little box of recipe cards.

II. Looting
That store window is only going to stay broken for so long.
The cops are on the way. So, I act with haste, grabbing
electronics, high-end sneakers and anything I can fence later.
There's obviously safety in numbers and in darkness, running
with looter laureates. The merchandise you leave unguarded
in conversation is fair game to me. You may call it grand
larceny and theft. I'm going to take as much as I can carry.

III. Dictation
The cardinals infiltrate the tree outside my bedroom window
each morning. I didn't coerce them; they found me. The muse
is tardy and full of excuses; I'll have to dock her pay. Half-
rhymes arrive on the nimbostratus. Imagery is like biblical
manna. It's just there in the morning, like tule fog in the
ditches of the Central Valley. Don't envy or pity me. I'm just the
underpaid secretary.

Breakaway Republics

Each word had broken out of its shell
\-   Bertolt Brecht

Think of the words
as independent entities,
with agency and vectors.

Words as citizenry,
each page a metropolitan statistical area,
or at least a borough.

Novelists speak of characters
who take on a life of their own,
insolence, sass and volition.

But what if this is also true
of the words?
You think you are writing

but you are merely
a federalist, a former Soviet
of breakaway republics:

Transnistira, Crimea,
Abkhazia, South Ossetia.
Etymology is cell biology;

poetics at the micron-level.
Imagine each word
as having a membrane,

a nucleus, ribosomes
and mitochondrion;
the basic unit of my life.

Ekphrasis - Visual Cues

I want to talk about an easy and proven source of prompts for poetry (and other lyrical genres like creative non-fiction)

The art of writing poetry about paintings is known as "ekphrasis" –a verbal description of a visual work of art, and that includes photography and sculpture.

I once wrote about an obscure bust in a storage wing of the Rodin Museum and have also written about Rodin's famous "Burghers of Calais" piece.

I was riding a bus in San Francisco's Chinatown a few years ago and saw the primary colors and grid patterns of a Mondrian painting in the assembled items in front of a hardware store.

Here are some other poet-painter poems:

Auden on Bruegel:
'Musée des Beaux Arts'

Sexton on Van Gogh
'The Starry Night', Anne Sexton

Langston Hughes on Winold Reiss
'I am the darker brother,'

Ginsberg on Cezanne
'Cezanne's Ports'

Emory University has a nice link to about 50 poems.

http://www.english.emory.edu/classes/paintings&poems/
titlepage.html

As an exercise, I decided to tackle one of my favorite pieces of art, a Marc Rothko painting that's at SFMOMA. The museum was closed for three years for renovation (most of the works traveled), but I made a visit on the last weekend of viewing in 2013 and that's the last time I stood in front of it; five years ago

What I like about writing a poem about a painting is I can describe the painting for you, and maybe drop in a little background about its origin, weave in a subtle bio of the painter, and also translate for you some kind of greater meaning or import.

The Rothko at SFMOMA

No. 14. 1960
is a nine-foot-tall

monolith and portal,
cathedral and chalice,

a burning coal-scape
red and orange over purple.

Is it the primal sunrise?
Is it a lover's final dusk?

Is it the love
I feel for my friends

And my children?
Or, does it express

a child's terror of what
it meant to be

Jewish in pogrom

Russia, to be blamed

for every misfortune?
In abstraction we dissolve.

From oil-on-canvas
we induce a fugue state

to strip away the names of things,
and speak only of numbers.

The Critique Group

Writing is such a solitary pursuit.

It's only natural that writers like to congregate in MFA programs, at bookstore readings, open mics., TEDx talks and in the social organism known as the writer critique group.

The ideal size for a critique group is five to six committed writers.

They must be willing to meet regularly, contribute consistently and critique fairly.

The main admonition I gave to the group is "don't critique someone else's work the way you would have written it. Make your critique organically. How can the piece become better based on the rules it sets out for itself?

Hopefully, this avoids stylistic differences and personal opinions and limits heavy-handed "here's how I would have handled that" advice.

I said, "hopefully." It's a hard row to hoe.

Another ideal state for a writer critique group is focus on a single genre. It's hard enough these days when writing is Balkanized into splinter groups like Military Science Fiction and Young Adult LGBT.

Can't we all just be regular Vanilla poets for one day? Do we have become breakaway republics championing sonnets, haiku and villanelles?

Another group dynamic is commitment. Writers drift in and out of group. Writers travel for work. Writers have families.

My most recent critique group met every other Monday afternoon at 5pm at a Starbucks in south Durham. I will give this group credit. I don't think anyone missed a Monday afternoon over the course of one year. Except "Veronica" (name changed), who had a heart attack one summer morning. I once flew all day from LAX to RDU, landed and made it to group on time.

You can also have tension when one member of the group starts to become published and popular, missing group because of a book tour or an agent meeting. It's time to cut that writer loose anyway. They don't need the group anymore.

I think the improv actor movie *Don't Think Twice* covers the fame theme quite nicely.

If you convene a group of creatives, eventually one or two members (out of six) is statistically going to have a run of artistic acceptance. Prepare for it.

I initiated and convened my group using Meet Up Raleigh, which has a larger pool of about 700 writers led by writer Tara Lynne Groth. I wanted to convene a Durham fiction group on the Northern end of the Triangle metro region, so we put the call out.

As group leader and an experienced, published writer, I get to set the rules. There's a natural deference from the less experienced writers:

"Marvin," a novelist, who makes his living as a realtor.

"Roberta" a Regency Romance author,

and the aforementioned "Veronica" a writing rookie and friend of Roberta.

It wasn't quite the hardcore, laser-focused literary fiction group I'd hoped for, but their loyalty was miles deep and the comments on my work were normally helpful and insightful.

I heard the story once of a group leader who had been kicked out of the group that this person had formed. I'm not sure of all the details but that had to be a juicy final meeting for the founder!

I'm also sure in other larger groups, couples form (and break-up) and a professional mediator with the wisdom of Solomon gets to determine which person gets custody of the critique group.

There are also minor conveniences. If you meet at someplace like a Starbuck's, you can't start until everyone has their coffee. So, if Writer A orders a regular coffee and Writer B orders a Mocha Caramel Latte with extra Mojo, then that's a problem.

Another issue is space. You walk into Starbucks and you have a group of four adult writers, none of them in their college blue jeans, if you get my drift. Where to sit? Invariably, there's a single scrapbooking girl or nebbish guy (complete with slide rule) rudely taking up an entire table, so the critique group is forced to cobble together a tiny table and nightstand and four rickety chairs in order to meet.

Said another way, most writers as a phylum, are too polite to evict the solo Starbuck's table squatter. I once had the idea of us all just sitting down at the single occupier, and launch into our writer talk to see if they would vamoose. I had no takers.

So, what is the exact benefit here?

The first bonus is having three other working stiff (or retired) writers as a motivational edge, adults who have families and household chores and DMV visits, who also find time to write.

Secondly, if you can work it out, you have three other people who absolutely love your preferred genre. Out of the general population, how often does that happen, to have three other humans who share your creative area of interest?

A third benefit is the insight. I call this the airport control tower effect. If you are flying an airplane, you are jammed into a tiny cockpit with all those instruments. The windshield is small and you can only see a limited square of what's ahead of you.

Your objective readers, on the other hand, have the 360-degree lofted view of the airfield and your plane. They can catch all the tiny errors, and the major miscues in your writing. And believe me, if you are critiquing their work, they won't miss anything!

I'm not sure you can get to Wilmette from the Loop in ten minutes.

Were Edsels even around in 1955?

And by the way, it was Ford, not GM, that manufactured them.

It's cummerbund, not cumberbundt. It's not a cake

The fourth benefit is continuity. These are the people who read that weakly-plotted crappy short story about your Korea trip. Or, they read the excellent first two chapters of that novel about nattily dressed robots, and wonder why you've not come back to writing anything of that quality since.

And best of all, these groups cost absolutely nothing to join or run, other than that $6 Mocha Caramel Latte, which makes you late anyway.

Sadly, my Durham fiction group is on hiatus. Roberta's daughter is having a baby, and Veronica wanted to work on her zydeco accordion skills. Unless Marvin and I want to sit there in the Starbuck's like Felix Ungar and Oscar Madison, we will need to go recruit other writers.

So, now on Monday afternoons between 5pm-7pm, I sit and write. The coffee is homemade drip but the table is quite spacious.

Le Mot Juste

Word choice is mostly about what you remove.

Word choice is about what you remove.

Word choice is about removal.

Remove words.

The average sentence is about 25 words long, and the average page of text is 250 words.

You can arguably make three passes through each sentence you write and remove one weak word on every pass. About 90% of what you wrote remains, but it will be more powerful.

"Brevity is the soul of wit," is an oft-repeated phrase you should think about when writing.

As a poet, I'm all about visual presentation. My line breaks are not random; they are intentional.

Lines of poetry are like mountain ledges protruding.

How far out can the poet venture on a line until it crumbles and the poet tumbles into the valley below?

We read down the page with a poem, but what we are really doing is ascending a cliff face, one handhold and piton at a time.

In prose, I'm not a fan of the ultra-long paragraph.

For the reader, it's an opaque gray blob that repels the eye and the mind. It's flabby with a dangerously high Body-Mass Index. It could be fatal to your story.

I'm a fan of the one-sentence paragraph.

It sits there isolated and naked on the page, a dynamo for my story.

A single sentence paragraph is a crooner in a leather jacket, leaning against a light post.

It's a lighthouse beam, sweeping the sea.

It's my dealer on the corner, waiting for a drop.

Now let's talk about the single word.

"Le Mot Juste" is term tossed about by English majors, poorly paid editors and book club hostesses, translating from the French as "the exact word."

Le mot juste is the perfect word that trips the tumbler, the key that activates the nuclear warheads of your prose.

Poets do not spray buckshot from a shotgun in hopes of hitting their prey with verbal volume.

Poets are snipers who can shatter a victim's back molars from two miles away while at the same time polishing the front teeth.

Take the precision required to work in the haiku form, the 5–7–5 syllable format, three lines with two main images and a kireji (cutting word) between them.

When you are counting syllables on your fingers, you are working in the base code of writing.

Haiku is far too precise for my taste. I admittedly play it loosely for the perfectionists.

Some people have Word of the Day calendars or subscribe to Word of the Day services. I don't find these organic enough for my writing; I want my new words to arise out of overheard speech, what I read, or my curiosity.

George Costanza on the sitcom Seinfeld was famous for throwing around big words like "anathema" or showing off cleverly in this exchange:

George: We had an incredible phone conversation. We talked for like twenty minutes. I thought she had a great voice timbre. Is it timbre or tamber?

Jerry: I think it's tamber.

George: Why'd I think it was timbre?

Jerry: I didn't notice the voice.

George: It's mellifluous!

I'm a lover of words, but not a show-off. I'd rather slip a word slyly into a poem or a sentence, subtly, and let it explode out of nowhere.

I'm hooked on the online etymology dictionary. Word origins fascinate me. It's like knowing the lineage of a racehorse, both the sire and the dam. "Sire" derives from "elder," and "dam" comes from "dame" and domus, the Latin word for house.

"Authentic" shares the same root as "author."

You might not have known that.

When you write, you express your authenticity.

Klutz – The Story of a Poem

In the spring of 1985, I finished my MFA in creative writing.
I was burned out. Two years of writing poetry and short stories and
presenting them in writing workshops for searing peer critique is
brutal. Don't try it.

I'd drained the well and the water table. For a year, I wrote nothing.

I went to work for a bank, in a back-office clerical role, processing
mortgage loan payoffs and cancelling deeds of trust. I was hardly
T.S. Eliot working for Lloyd's; far from it. Plus, I had no Pound or
Hemingway to arrange a private fund so I could escape from my day
job.

And then one night I was washing dishes and this poem arrived:

The Klutz

The sink narrows like a vise,
and the wineglass I'm washing
pings against the porcelain sink,
sprinkling shards into the suds.
I assume a constant state
of genuflection, retrieving
pills, pens, coins: they flee
my grasp like Mexican jumping
beans. Please do not ask me
to carry the groceries, hang
pictures, dust the mantle. I
succumb to indexterity.
Made for the moon maybe?
Where everything fragile
gives a second chance,
and the Blue Delft figurine
knocked from the counter
floats over my fingertips,
whirling above gravity,
a dervish of the divine.

If you have ever felt like objects in the physical world are working against you, you will certainly appreciate a kitchen sink that "narrows like a vise" and futile attempts to hang an uncooperative picture or dust elusive figurines on the mantle.

The poem also looks for some form of "divine" intervention, where gravity might suspend and the wineglass stays in one piece for another day.

I also had fun with the self-deprecating title, from the Yiddish klots meaning "clumsy person, blockhead," which derives from the Middle High German klotz "lump, ball."

There is humor and wit in the piece, and domestic insight (please don't ask me to do household chores that we both know will result in something broken!). The poet speaks to himself, and perhaps to an adjacent spouse who shakes her head in dismay.

The poet, in wondering if he is made for the moon, admits he may not be entirely at home on this planet or in his house.

There's also a spiritual subtext here, as the poet speaks of genuflection, and a zen-like acceptance, succumbing to the minor god, indexterity.

At twenty lines, this blank verse poem reminds me a bit of a sonnet. A more accomplished poet might have been able to pull it off in one of the classic sonnet forms: Petrarchan, Shakespearian or Spenserian. But I'm not that guy and I know I'm not that guy.

"The Klutz" has its moments and I'm glad the editors of *Tar River Poetry* concurred when they published it a year later.

The Reading

- For Dawn Reno Langley

I've been making a list of the things they don't teach you at school.
They don't teach you how to love somebody or what to say to
somebody who is dying. They don't teach you how to be famous.
- Neil Gaiman

I.
The college schedules the reading for early Friday evening, in
a small North Carolina town where you used to live in, an hour
away; Friday, the 13th as it happens. There will be a small musical
program, and then the focus will be on you, the headliner.

This reading, while welcome, messes with your Friday routine. You
pack a cardboard box with thirty copies your latest novel. You go
to the bank to get one-dollar bills, in case people want to buy the
book and only have a twenty-dollar bill. If you sold each copy for
$20, instead of $16, your life would be easier. You wouldn't have to
make change all the time.

You stop work on your current manuscript around 3 p.m., shower,
get dressed, and make a snack in the kitchen. It's only an hour
away but there will be Friday afternoon traffic to navigate. There
always a lot of trucks on that highway you recall, gravel trucks and
tractor trailer semis bound for Wal-Mart.

The drive north is quite lovely, here in early April. The red buds
are out, and some dogwoods. The city landscape of bright, gaudy
strip malls and impervious surface turns to countryside. The farms,
meadows and ponds are a welcome change from your suburban
environs at home. You pass an expansive solar energy field and
remember when it was just a handful of experimental panels, a
patchwork of mirrors on the sloping cow pasture.

Overall, you are feeling good about things and you are productive;
make that prolific. You have no end to ideas for future projects.
Your novel is selling well and you are getting decent reviews. It's

also leading to interest from agents and publishers in your next book.

Your self-funded book tour of the lower forty-eight states last summer helped, the power of a grassroots movement, hosted by independent bookstores. A local book club in Hillsborough hosted you in January: they baked a cake in the shape of an elephant (one of the main characters in the novel) and the group presented you with an elephant-themed blank journal at the end of the evening; sweet and completely disarming.

       II.

This reading is sponsored by a small community college. Your former staff and colleagues greet you warmly. A student (deputized) carries your cardboard box of novels for sale into the room where you will read. His oxford dress shirt is un-tucked in the back you notice. All the student ambassadors are wearing the oxford dress shirts, with khaki trousers, the school logo embroidered on the left side of the dress shirt.

The room where you will read is small and windowless, set up with rows of yellow chairs with padded seats and backs. The lighting is fluorescent; not your favorite. At least they have a podium, black polished metal. It resembles a high-tech music stand.

There's an event in the next room, a student a Capella group. The talent level is delightful. You recognize the popular tune; they are transforming it with this arrangement. In the Bible Belt you're going to find an endless depth of exceptional singers and harmonizers; thank the churches for that one. The other room is packed, with parents and siblings of the performers. You recognize the new college president in the front row; you haven't met her yet but you've heard good things.

The performance ends and there are refreshments: punch and Chilean grapes and cheddar cheese cubes.

Several women drift into your room and take seats in the

middle rows, avoiding the front. A dean from the college introduces you. The college publicist wanders in and takes two photos for posterity. You never see the college president that evening.

The reading goes well. You read two short chapter excerpts, so the audience gets a feeling for two of the main characters, including the elephant. One woman has brought her ten-year-old daughter, who is in a colorful pink and purple dress and wearing an oversized hair bow. You remember her as an infant, and read the elephant chapter straight to her, as if it's a bedtime story.

The Q&A is surprisingly evolved. This is a literate community, when they make the effort. You sell two copies of the novel and the deputized student carries the near-full box of novels back to your car.

III.
Four people on a Friday night is a shame. You sense the college didn't quite promote you enough. They could have at least made it mandatory for English majors.

You are an author with fifteen books, national journal publications, awards and a small following in Denmark and the Netherlands, environmentalists mostly.

Seen another way, an audience of four is a blessing. There's an intimacy and a connection about it. Your friend's daughter might become a writer, a voice, because of this evening. People who didn't make it, at least knew you were in town.

IV.
At a stoplight, you run into a former colleague from the biology department. He is in a bright-yellow basketball jersey that says "Teachers" and apologizes for missing you; Friday night intramural play and he is their star rebounder.

You drive by your old house at dusk. The front door is painted purple. They've removed your roses from the front. You remember the sunroom in back, where you wrote your second book, a collection of essays. This town, a Mayberry, came at a good time in your life. Your daughter finished high school and you got off her into a decent college without any drama or tragedy.

The drive back on the highway is restorative. There's a classic car show in the vast parking lot in front of the bowling alley. The solar farm panels are now silver-blue, reflecting twilight. The roadside ponds appear dark and bottomless.

The good news here is you'll be home earlier than you thought, and refreshed from the getaway to the northern edge of the state.

There's time to make a cup of tea and write for a few hours. The next book beckons.

Obits

*I have never killed a man, but I have read many obituaries with
great pleasure.*
- Clarence Darrow

I.
You're supposed to read the local obituaries every day to make
sure you're not in there.

I lived in Greensboro, North Carolina for 28 years, and my morning
ritual (after coffee and a shave) is a scan of the obituaries in the
News & Record online edition. On occasion, I will take a look at the
Independent in Santa Barbara, where I was born and lived until I
was twenty-five-years old. I don't bother with the Durham Sun; I
hardly know anyone here.

When I worked for the Hearst paper The Chronicle in San
Francisco several years ago, I was the project manager for a
complete makeover of the obituary page, which we rebranded as
"Life Tributes." John Miller led the redesign and I worked with the
ad sales department on a repackaging of the obituary product. It
was a multi-million dollar business, and the average charge was
$1,100 for a print obituary, that came pre-bundled with an online
obituary on SFGate.

What astounded me was the Sunday factor. If you died on a
Tuesday, the family would purchase a brief death notice for
Wednesday and wait to run the full biography obituary on Sunday.
Sometimes we had about six pages of obituaries in what is known
as the "lean back" edition that you leisurely read on a Sunday.

Even if Giuseppe or Juanita lived (and died) out in Walnut Creek
(Rossmoor) or Livermore, if they grew up in the City, the old San
Francisco families made sure to run a full obituary in the San
Francisco Newspaper.

Consider the absolute power of the obituary, as one's final edition on the planet. Woe to the newspaper that messed up an obituary with a typo, or God forbid, the wrong photo. No retraction or refund could possibly undo the dishonor of a gaffe-ridden obituary read by 600,000 souls (print edition); it was like a typo on the tombstone.

And if you were famous, the Op-Ed editors wrote an obituary about you that cost the family nothing at all. What determined famous versus "pay to play" I'll never know, but it was some algorithm or Egyptian hieroglyph that only the graduates of Stanford Journalism School or Cal are privy to. I'm sure there are many widows and publicists who walked out of 901 Mission Street in a tizz because their beloved or their client did not rate the editorial obituary.

Robin Williams died while I worked at the Chronicle. What I realized with his passing is that there are no more news bureaus anymore. We were the sole source of news for the entire world. Our Managing Editor created a War Room and detailed 18 reporters to Tiburon and Sea Cliff to cover the passing of Mork from Ork (and my favorite, Mrs. Euphengenia Doubtfire.)

II.
Any writer worth his embalming fluid should read the local obituaries religiously. They're an unending source of rich material.

Each obituary is an encapsulated memoir, written on-the-fly, drafted the backside of a Mel's Diner menu or the mortuary's price list.

I wrote my father's obituary on Labor Day Weekend 2009 in concourse C of the Charlotte airport, as I flew out to Phoenix to meet my sisters to have his body cremated.

I'm fascinated with the process by which grieving family members convene, and the most literate member is deputized as the scribe, plus the supporting roles: Uncle Josiah, you fact check, and Cousin Ginny, you proofread.

An obituary is a lovely genre, a prose poem of 300-900 words
written in haste and grief: essential facts (birthdate and place); an
abridged highlight reel of accomplishments (career, domestic and
civic); and for the outro, a compact genealogy (don't forget the
step-grandchildren!)

What incredible material for the writer to use for plotting and
characterization!

And you don't really have to ask anyone's permission. It runs in the
newspaper and you're not really going to plagiarize anything; most
likely adapt it or use it as a starting point for a short story, memoir
or novel.

What intrigues me the most is in the cases of divorced couples, if
the former spouse is listed as a survivor, especially if the deceased
re-married.

I like to curate names from obituaries as names for characters (for
example Merchant LeRoy, Wartha Delano, from the Greensboro
paper).

With the Santa Barbara obituaries, I can instantly return to
the family names and scenarios of my childhood. Who needs
madelienes when you have the Mass for the dead notice right
there in front of you as a trigger?

And with the Greensboro paper, these are most likely the people
that I knew while in my middle-aged years, when I was working
at the bank and raising a family. Sometimes it's their parents or
siblings passing.

I usually learn something new about the person or family that I did
not previously. Death is the final correction.

III.
Many newspaper editorial departments have a file full of prewritten
obituaries for famous people, and when they die, the writer merely

updates the facts on the Internet or by phone, and sends the fresh piece over to the copy editor.

In the case of a national celebrity like Robin Williams with an unexpected and controversial death (how did he die exactly?), the pre-fab obituary gets to "live" on for several news cycles, and maybe a follow-up story in three months.

Given the certainty of one's mortality and the unknown time of arrival, should you pre-write your own obituary?

James Joyce thought this was a good idea. He suggested that the perspective of writing your own obituary would "give you a second wind."

I have not taken this step. I'm single these days, and I will count on my daughters and my friends to come up with a pithy piece on short order, the same way I had to do it when my father passed away. I say, don't hesitate; write the thing before my body goes cold.

And if you get stuck, just crib from the dust jacket of one of my books. I won't mind.

As a memoirist, I've already set out the kindling wood. The three memoirs I've written (so far) are in essence long-form obituaries that will live forever and ever on Amazon, Amen.

Density

In my mid to late thirties, I struggled to make a consistent living as I transitioned out of banking. Boring bank work had been perfect, stable work for me as a "Steady Eddie" husband and father, but with all the bank mergers in the mid 1990's, the field had become chaotic and unpredictable.

As a liberal arts major with an MFA in creative writing, I had quickly learned the accounting and finance basics necessary to make consumer and commercial loans and run a bank branch profit center. Now I was having to adapt and pivot yet again, learning sales, marketing and operations and information technology, competing with MBA's in the Greensboro job market.

I occasionally reviewed fiction for the Greensboro News & Record (books by Alice Munro, Charles Frazier, Sara Gruen). I wrote nothing creatively from 1996 to 2004. I just wasn't interested.

As my energy went into my career, my creativity went underground like a river.

I wrote and published a few poems, and that was it. Terri and I took a long weekend trip to New Orleans for our 10th wedding anniversary. I captured one evening in the French Quarter in poem called "Density" which The Greensboro Review published it in 1997.

It's a solid poem, and it speaks to the energy I feel in large cities, where everything is so texturally rich and compact. Each block is packed with a thousand details and secrets, pressed down like layers of sediment in a river. And it's dense and ultra-sensitive, like the taste buds on your tongue.

I also wanted to capture the culinary elegance of having dinner in the French Quarter. At this restaurant, you felt incredibly wealthy. There was an temporary extravagance about it, a fleeting lavishness. We were a two-hour, non-stop flight from home, but worlds away.

Like most of my poems, it is visual and cinematic. The poet is almost like a filmmaker's camera panning across the scene, and in this poem, going through a wall to see what's on the other side, gawking at an upstairs window in a courtyard and wondering what the story is.

There is mystery and marvel, and tiny short story about being in New Orleans, in the aftermath of Mardi Gras, when everything shuts down.
It is also a parable of our marriage: we are ten years in, could still have delightful times, but we did not know what was around the corner.

Density (Vieux Carre)

A row of corn-fed hens twirl on a spit,
the flames feeding on garlic and olive oil
rubbed deep into the skin. Here,

under the cotton tent. Here, under clouds
that glide overhead like a river, gliding
over the star river bottom. Here,

in a courtyard restaurant on Decatur,
a block from the river, the owner
leases the lease from another, and so does

the guy upstairs. He rents a single room above
the cooler holding duck, lamb, rib eye, gulf fish
and veal. You can see the blue glow of his TV

on a wall, and maybe that's the shadow of a chair
or it's his back as he's bending over. The waitress
says he keeps his wild girlfriend locked up there.

So, maybe the wall behind your copper-flashed hair
hides a family of fifteen from Estonia or Eritrea,

a parking garage, or the garret

where Faulkner wrote "Soldier's Pay." At the corner
there's a dumpster filled with construction debris
and topped with Mardi Gras waste:

wallboard and tile, pipe, plaster and fiberglass,
go cups, broken necklaces, and soggy masks. During
Lent, everything slows down. And here,

on a wide moon of plate, the roasted onion rests
in the sauce's rich reduction. On a red pepper tongue,
a thousand taste buds wait.

Stories

Write a short story every week. It's not possible to write 52 bad short stories in a row.
- Ray Bradbury

I'm primarily a poet. Short fiction is a graft onto the lyrical tree, and it shows.

I blame early success in the genre. A short story I wrote when I was 23 years old "Not Really Mine to Give," won Second Place in the Santa Barbara News & Review fiction competition. The story that one first place in the contest was a Vietnam story of inferior quality. But you are not going to beat a Vietnam story with a mediocre Raymond Carver derivative story in 1982. There's no way.

I read short stories in The New Yorker and The Atlantic and Granta, and developed aspirations. I enrolled in fiction workshops in graduate school (a classmate was about to have a story in Best American Short Stories, 1984.) My M.F.A. thesis in 1985 consisted of four short stories and a long narrative poem, but I really didn't know what I was doing.

The short stories in my M.F.A. thesis were not "slice of life" pieces; they were languid "lumps of life." They were linguine, and not exactly al dente. Those four stories had no plotting whatsoever, and limited dialogue.

But I did salvage one of the stories "The Winter Practice," for my debut story collection in 2016. By salvage I mean rescuing it from the deep, with scuba divers, two cranes and a barge. I added a lyrical introduction and layered in several plot lines.

I began intentionally writing short stories when we moved to Briarcliff Road in Greensboro in 1986, and four stories from that period were published.

Greensboro was the hometown of the infamous short story writer O.Henry (formerly William Sydney Porter). I knew some of the Porter descendants. It was a cultural mandate that I learn to write in Porter's preferred genre, while also avoiding his contrived, clever endings.

Some stories from the Briarcliff (Jurassic) Era, I printed out and placed in three-ring binders and some were saved on floppy disks. Most of the stories from then longer exist, due to a series of hasty moves I made between 2011 and 2016, two of them cross-country. I suspect the majority of those proto-stories are now in a St. Petersburg, Florida landfill overlooking I-275.

In 1987, I wrote a story about my former roommate, a free spirit busker/troubadour nicknamed "Brick," who drove the shuttle van for a church Sunday school. I made sure he got into lots of trouble taking a single divorcee home, the final passenger in the van. I recall something involving a sneeze shield at a Shoney's salad bar. The story was titled "The Bus Ministry."

Later that year I wrote a short story (title unknown) about domestic maids in Greensboro's Irving Park neighborhood that might remind you of the 2011 movie, The Help. I was ahead of my time.

A few stories that remain intact, and you can find these four on Amazon in my first short story collection, The Winter Practice:

Stories come from weird places. I had a roommate who worked for a funeral home. To talk his way out of a traffic ticket, my roommate's boss, the head undertaker, made my roommate lie down in the back of the funeral transport van, where bodies going to autopsy are carried. I converted this into an uncle-nephew buddy story, switched the setting and made the whole thing a road trip to Asheville. I sent "Hot Dog" to John Miller on a whim, and he published it in Equator in 1987, my first national publication.

I read about a soldier's body found in a melting glacier, and imagined events which might have precipitated that in pre-World War II Hungary. Hungary was a random choice, but had a vague Eastern European ambience. I told the tale from the point of view of the soldier's son. North Carolina author Clyde Edgerton selected "Confessions of a Pacifist" as one of the six winner stories in the N.C. Writers Network Fiction Syndication Competition. The story ran in four North Carolina newspapers in 1988.

I wrote about working part-time in the Stang's pharmacy in downtown Greensboro in a story called "Smile, It's Your Wedding Day!" Tom Keely included that in his new journal, Cities and Roads. In the story, a pharmacy assistant gets married on her lunch hour to a graduate student and returns to work to find that the pharmacist has splurged on a deli tray of cold cuts and the sundries manager is freely pouring the discount soda in celebration. It's a fun, cinematic story.

I had a strange experience at a family friend's funeral and I turned that into the final scene of "The Mystery of My Mother." The story is not about my mother, but told from the perspective of my former wife recounting escapades of her mother. Marsha Van Hecke selected the story for inclusion in the Greensboro anthology, O.Henry Festival Stories 1989

I've written over 60 short stories in the past 35 years, with most of them on Amazon in my two collections, The Winter Practice and Centripetal Force, and a dozen or more under construction in the fiction garage.

I'll often write the story in one sitting (five or fifteen pages), and then I might let the thing sit for a while.

In fairness I'm an A+ poet, and a B+ short story writer, although the semester's not over yet. As you would imagine, the prose is lyrical but I'm less proficient with plot, character and dialogue.

I write stories mostly because I have always loved reading short stories, going back to John Updike, John Cheever, Raymond

Carver Frederick Barthelme, Breece D'J Pancake and Richard Ford, and forward to my current favorites like Alice Munro, William Trevor, Wells Tower and Tessa Hadley.

I think back to those writing sessions at Briarcliff Road, composing in longhand (or on my Smith Corona electric typewriter) in the den that the realtors think is a third bedroom.

Some neighborhood kids are skateboarding recklessly down Northwood Street without even stopping at the intersection. Our cat Chloe is using the litter box in the bathroom, Katherine is watching Barney or Raffi or The Lion King out on the sun porch and Terri (pregnant with Lizzi) is making the best of our galley kitchen and whipping up beef stroganoff or clam chowder. Domestic bliss!

Panhandling for Poets

I'm going to stand in the rain
outside the Regulator Bookshop
on 9th Street with a cardboard
sign and beg you for words,
for anything approximating
syntax, for all forms of
plot twist and happenstance.

I'm going to stand there
as a self-proclaimed Veteran,
with two-day stubble
and threadbare threads,
shaking you down there
for my rightful inheritance
of denouement, digression
and deus ex machina.

Maybe another time, you say,
As if in a rejection notice,
Going round me
And plunking down good
money instead for a bright
golden box of Do-si-do's
(Oatmeal and Peanut Butter)
from the Girl Scouts
in the courtyard.

I am cipher, ellipsis,
The errata of your errands;
single apostrophe
where a letter used to be.

Dossier

Note: Sources include former associates of our firm, and informants cultivated over many years from our work in satellite states and puppet regimes. Names of personages herein have been altered to protect the identity and safety of the informants.

1. The Poet was observed at a grocery establishment known as Food Panther (Belgian ownership), aggregating an amalgam of healthy (cucumber, spinach) and unhealthy (liberal New England "Triple Chunk" ice cream) items. Tripwire: The Poet paid with hard currency, bills and declined to use a loyalty card, i.e. paid full price for all items. This is an obvious attempt to stay off the grid and avoid tracking.

2. During the colder winter months, The Poet does not leave his domicile for days on end. He will emerge on occasion, to return books and movie DVD's to the local library, aka "Drop #2." The Poet picks up items that have been placed "on hold." We request additional funding to investigate Librarians #37 and #52, former residents of Bosnia-Herzegovina and Burkina Faso, respectively.

3. A former girlfriend of The Poet ("Susan") describes his bizarre methodology of perusing library DVD's. He will watch the movie in its entirety (Disc #1) and then watch the Special Features (Disc #2), then return to Disc #1 and watch the movie for a second time. Many of these films "("Giant" "Splendor in the Grass" "Cat on a Hot Tin Roof") can be watched easily on the classic movie cable channel. Why go to all this trouble? Our analysts suspect that breached data may be embedded in the Director's Commentary or the subtitles.

4. The Poet is observed at a local Stardollars (corporate store #5747), every other Monday at 5 p.m. for a "writing critique group." Our experience suggests this is a common tool of espionage, the literary sleeper cell, where encoded data from the aforementioned classic movies are shared in "short stories" that are distributed among group members. The critique group members include

Miguel, age 52 (alias Muscle Mike, aka Mikhail Rostov), Jennifer, age 32, and the prolific Estelle V., age 72, an author who self-publishes Regency Romances and young adult science fiction. The cell members were recruited in January, from a Continuing Education writing workshop at a local community college, an obvious and albeit laughable spycraft tactic.

5.   Through our associate Megan (a local university coed), we have infiltrated a local independent bookstore, which sponsors a monthly "open mic" event. There is a sign-up sheet and The Poet always arrives early and enrolls as Reader #6 for the evening. Some would see this as humility and reticence of a shy poet who doesn't want to be the lead-off act. In our analysis, the number six (aka "seis" aka "sechs") has long been associated with literary terrorism and we fully expect escalation of activity in the month of June, especially June 6th, at 6 p.m., which is interestingly the next open mic event. Please note that Megan would like some financial assistance for the books she has had to purchase with her "employee discount." (see our April invoice, line 37)

6.   Good news. Our librarians have agreed to become informants. They are suggesting that there might be encrypted messages in the library's "late notices," and that The Poet intentionally keeps books beyond the due date, in order to trigger the download. Additionally, he pays his overdue fines with small change, another form of signaling.

7.   We're onto him now. The Poet is a consistent contributor to literary journals, many of them run out of university English Departments, and we all know what that means. In our previous employ running the Liberal Arts desk at Langley, these literary journals and associated M.F.A. programs are well-documented hotbeds for nefarious activity. Our assertion here is that The Poet is intentionally writing subgrade poems in order to receive rejection notices, which contain encrypted instructions to activate the Stardollar sleeper cell. The standard rejection notice phrasing "we hope you will re-submit your work at another time," is both insincere and blatant in its encouragement of impending sabotage.

8.   A setback. Megan has experienced a decline in her GPA due to her assignment at the independent bookstore. Her parents are asking her to cut back her hours (surveillance) until she has resumed her spot on the Dean's List. In the meantime, Megan continues to seek reimbursement for any and all self-help books and coffee table books obtained with her employee discount. We request your immediate attention to this matter, thank you.

9.   The Poet is overheard at Stardollars by our embedded barista, speaking to Miguel and Jennifer of "agents" and "deadlines." We do not believe these should be taken at face value as the lingua franca of unpublished authors.

10. The critique group sleeper cell appears to be disbanding. Estelle V. is leaving to help with a new granddaughter (also a Megan) in Port Royal, VA, which has huge geographical implications for our project. As you know from your history, Port Royal was the final hold-out for the nefarious John Wilkes Booth, and is certainly symbolic. At this final meeting, The Poet paid for his "Americano" with loose change and was last seen headed to the library with a stack of overdue DVD's, mostly films by Douglas Sirk (alias Hans Detlef Sierck), a German national. We will let you draw your own conclusions.

Learning to Surf (Campus Point)

I have wandered through this world
As each moment has unfurled
I've been waiting to awaken from these dreams.
- Jackson Browne, Doctor My Eyes

Writing about the writing life is a necessity, as much as making sure I get out of my house and walk in Eno River State Park and hike the trails. It has to be done.

My book Myriad had its genesis in several conversations I had with people who were considering taking their writing more seriously, members of my Monday night Panera fiction group who are writing novels, and with others in mind who might be exploring the creative writing arena.

Like Faulkner, you write because you enjoy it and take satisfaction in storytelling and manipulating language in interesting ways. If you're in it for the money or the glory, this is not your book. There's a good deal of discipline and perseverance involved, but at the end of the day, you may only have a handful of loyal readers and your royalty check won't buy you a steak dinner, and by that I mean hamburger steak.

Several years ago, my wise friend Jack Whitley introduced me to screenwriter Steven Pressfield's fine book "The War of Art: Break Through the Blocks and Win Your Inner Creative Battles." After you finish this book, you should order that one.

At this point in my life, approaching my seventh decade on the planet, I have been writing creatively for 40 years and professionally for 15 years. Time served, as they say.

My professional writing phase followed the events of 9/11, and a subsequent divorce, long stretch of unemployment and chapter 7 bankruptcy filing, and a complete leveling of my career. My good friend John Miller got me hired me to write the Ringling Brothers annual circus program in Tampa in December 2002 and I haven't looked back.

Interestingly, my creative output surged following an ischemic stroke in 2015. In about a year, I pulled together six books of poetry, fiction and memoir, much of it new material. These major life events have a way of "reshuffling the deck" as my artist friend Anne Willson observed.

I have a Master's degree in Creative Writing, what is known as a "studio degree." While UNC Greensboro is not Iowa or Columbia, I consider it one of the best writing programs in the country for the attention I received and the quality of the faculty.

I've self-published six books of creative work. I've ghostwritten eight business books for clients, on topics ranging from cloud computing (2010) to artificial intelligence/machine learning (2017). I've written and published in just about every creative genre, but have not yet finished a novel, a screenplay or a stage play.

I 've been around the block enough times. I had something to say. I was writing poems about writing poems, and posting motivational quotes from famous writers on my Facebook page. It was time to step up.

Maybe you're exploring your potential as a writer, or tinkering in a format like a poem or short story, or thinking about writing a novel. My premise here is: you're not becoming a Writer, or writing (insert genre); it's more subtle than that. It's a writing life, indivisible from whom you are. You live it, and breathe it, at your desk, at the coffee shop, or when you are driving down the road. Writing infuses you and lights a fuse.

"I'm going to approach this book by guessing some of the questions you may have now, anticipating questions that will come to you as you explore expressing yourself in creative formats.

What is it to write a poem, a short story or a full-blown novel?

Is it okay if I don't use rhyme or meter in a poem?

How is a short story different from a novel?

What degree of solitude is required to push past the forces that will resist my creative efforts?

How do I even begin to write about a particular place or a person or an idea in a clear and compelling way, that grabs the attention of a reader, a publisher, an agent or my Aunt Sophie?

Should I enroll in an M.F.A. creative program or just write on my own?"

I'll begin by telling you a story about how I learned to surf.

I began surfing in Southern California when I was 12 years old. Near the campus of U.C Santa Barbara and the small town of Isla Vista, there is a beginner's break known as Campus Point. At the entrance to campus, there was a guard house and a perfect place for Dad's to drop off sons and surfboards on their way to work: have fun, see you at 6pm.

Unlike much of the coastline, the bottom at Campus Point is sandy and the only treacherous rocks (and foot slicing barnacles) are up at the tip of the point, where experienced surfers paddle out. Further down the point, the waves break gentler, there are fewer surfers and it's easier to get the hang of balancing on a moving surfboard that wants to tip you off it four different ways (front, back and both sides).

This is where I learned to surf. The broken part of the wave is called the whitewater. It was very forgiving and I didn't get in anyone's way.

Despite the mellow nature portrayed in "Fast Times at Ridgemont High" surfers are very territorial and don't like having to avoid rookie surfers when traversing a wave. The pejorative term for this is a "geek."

You don't want to be a geek in the line-up. You want to learn your skills far from the madding crowd, and move up when you're ready.

This book is intended to be a Campus Point for new writers.

Not necessarily, young writers, but anyone who is interested in writing seriously in creative genres. My job is to get your comfortable with the basics, and then later on you can tackle the more challenging surf spots like Pipeline on the north shore of

Oahu and Teahupoo in Tahiti.

Writing at 60

Never tease an old dog; he might have one bite left.
- Robert A. Heinlein

Old age isn't a battle: old age is a massacre.
-Philip Roth

I.
Older than Dirt

Methuselah.

Move it, Gramps.

Have you saved enough for retirement?

I've fallen and I can't get up

We've been dreading our elderliness our entire lives and now it's here, dagnabit. Let the Geriatric Games begin.

Infirmities abound. I'm awake three times each night doing the enlarged-prostate-shuffle and the first five steps out of bed are zombie-like, my knees creak, the floorboards creak and the even the creaks creak.

II.
The AARP solicitations start coming in the mail when you're 50 and it pisses you off, slightly. Rock stars from your adolescence keel over, seemingly in batches.

Your metabolism not only slows, it goes negative on you so you gain weight when you eat nothing all day.

Welcome to Ice Station Six Zero, your Seventh Decade on the planet.

You can actually see Social Security in the distance, a mirage from Lawrence of Arabia. If you're lucky, there's a well and a bucket waiting for you, but probably not a palm tree or shade.

I'm lucky for a writer. I'm single, an empty nester and I've already figured out how to live on not very much income, in anticipation of not much income.

I'm not freaking out that I've saved nothing for my retirement. My retirement funding was wiped out in triplicate: 2002, 2008 and 2015.

This late-in-life austerity means freedom. I write for clients about half the day (or half the week), and the other half I work on

my own writing projects. And with three distinct fallow periods of creativity (the late 1980's, the mid 1990's and early aughts), I have quite a bit unwritten.

III.
Unfortunately, the list of books I want to write grows longer, the more books I finish.

I blog on Medium. I blog on LinkedIn. I post new poems on Facebook.

I turn old poems into flash fiction and extract poems from old short stories. I have this massive unsightly junkyard out back which has innumerable Ford and Honda chassis to strip for parts.

I have a sense of urgency that most do not.

I had an ischemic stroke in 2015 at age 57, and almost died. I've participated in hospital stroke survivor support groups, and I have seen first-hand how debilitating that cholesterol-caused event could have been. Luckily my stroke was 100% motor skill damage; I was cracking jokes in the ER as they took me off for a CT scan and an MRI.

I made puns from my neurologist's last name even as she took scissors to my new polo shirt from Target on the ER table.

"This is a Nguyen-Nguyen situation for me, isn't it Doc?

She didn't laugh. She's not supposed to.

The only thing bad about motor skill damage is I had to learn to walk again, speak clearly and type again with my left hand. I still can't bar chord on my guitar the way I used to. But all my cognitive functioning is there, and the old black bullwhip (wit) can still snap at the speed it used to.

My one danger is a tendency for manic behavior, and what my therapist diagnosed as a personality disorder, that sound like Single A-Fresno form of Tourette's, an inability to read and process social cues and keep my weird thoughts and musings to myself.

I'm not officially in the workforce and I haven't insulted anyone lately.

IV.
I hope I have a novel in me. I've started a novel in early 2017 and hope to finish it this year.

I have some ancestral memoirs/creative nonfiction I would like to work on some family books:

* my grandmother's childhood on the Alberta prairie
* my Irish ancestors leaving Ireland to come to Canada
* my great-great grandfather Welty, the Civil War cavalry captain
(PA 18th) who rode with Averill's Raiders in the Shenandoah,
met Kit Carson and spent the last half of his life as a newspaper
publisher in Vidalia, Indiana.

There's also a Steinbeck book I want to adapt into a documentary or biopic screenplay.

I have a series, a spoof of Sacramento called Mentos that I want to develop for Netflix. Think Portlandia but with mullets and a Led Zeppelin soundtrack.

Lately, I've become enamored with writing flash fiction, little 1,000-word vignettes.

And more poems, many more poems.

V.
I had a college friend my age die suddenly this past year. Paul was on the highway driving home from work, suffered a heart attack, and slowly drifted to the highway shoulder, harming no one.

My father died at age 73, in a Phoenix Arizona neuro hospital, with my sister Joy by his side. I was lucky enough to visit with him after his initial stroke (hemorrhagic) and I watched in the ICU as he came out of a three-day coma.

I know the longer I stick around, the more of my friends will start dying over the next decade. I don't need an actuarial table to know that.

The world ends not with a bang or a whimper. It will be a nurse following a DNR request and pulling a tube out someone's throat, or it will be a final steak dinner with twice-baked potato, pureed in a blender, and served with a straw.

Roth was right: it will be a massacre. Hopefully, I'll be around to write to about it.

Mirror Mortals

I.
Consider the common mirror, also known as a reflecting or looking glass. It's from the Latin *mirare*, to look at.

There are also several related words, like *admiration* and (stretch) *miracle*?

There's a Narcissistic quality to a mirror, one that flatters the ego. It is quite simply, a proof of existence.

Socrates is said to have urged young people to look at themselves in mirrors. If they were beautiful, they should become worthy of their beauty, and if they were ugly, they would know to hide their disgrace through learning. Mirrors are responsible for the first community colleges and schools that teach appliance repair.

I've always liked the mirror metaphor in Paul's first letter to the Corinthians, chapter 13: For now we see in a mirror dimly, but then face to face.

Mirrors have been used for divination since biblical times. It's considered bad luck to break one. To prove you are alive, you fog a mirror.

We frame mirrors and create instant portraiture. We produce full-length mirrors, in order to view our entire body of work in one glance.

Our first mirrors were ponds or pools of water. Then came obsidian, volcanic glass, followed by metallic mirrors made from bronze, copper and tin.

It was the 13th-century Venetian glassmakers on the glassy island of Murano who came up with the idea of plate glass. And 400 years later, the French used an industrial process for mirror making involving mercury, which unfortunately killed off many of the mirror workers.

Today's standard aluminum glass mirror is made of float glass using a vacuum coating, aluminum powder is "sputtered" onto a piece of glass.

II.
This book has been a process of holding up a mirror to my writing.

I wanted to see for myself in Socratic terms if there was beauty, or if I should go back to school.

My core talent is poetry, which can be a substrate skill involved in writing fiction, memoir and plays.

The poet's love of language, and lyrical deployment can elevate standard prose. Taken to an extreme, that lyricism ends up as flowery and overly wrought; of trying too hard.

Additionally, the poet must learn characterization and plot and have an ear for dialogue, which are often challenges the poet cannot surmount. But even in failure, the experience of ranging into other genres. The poet's next chapbook is marked by peopled poems and dramatic monologues, where the speakers spout witty snippets of dialogue, and the free verse follows a more pronounced narrative arc.

Said another way, if you live in Napa or France for a year, you're going to come away from that twelve-month immersion a better herb gardener, chef and sommelier, even if no one ever hires you in that official capacity.

III.
My other intention with this book-length mirror experiment was to reflect upon what it is like to live one's writing day in and day out.

Writing for used to be an avocation, something pursued as a sideline. I "kept my day job" and wrote at night and on weekends, and on vacation.

A few years ago, a series of Lemony Snicket-style incidents, normally devastating, allowed me to morph into a half-time writer.

I found Stephen Pressfield's "The War of Art" quite helpful as I made this transition. It helped me breakthrough creatively and take my writing more seriously. I learned to approach my own writing as professionally as I did ghostwriting a book for a client on artificial intelligent or project management.

As Somerset Maugham famously said, "I write only when inspiration strikes. Fortunately it strikes every morning at nine o'clock sharp."

IV.
I'm a grinder. I like to believe that luck follows on the heels of preparation, like a puppy following its master around the kitchen.

I wrote some really superb poems in my early twenties, and as I approach sixty, I believe my writing is as strong as it's ever been.

I'm not sure if I'm on the cusp of anything great. I may end up writing "more of the same" for the next decade. I'm hoping to have a few more literary journal publications before I'm through. It's a very sporadic and random pursuit, and I tend to "shotgun" my work out into the litsphere, and hope for a break from screeners and a hook into the final editor.

Acceptance letters are wonderful. "We really like your work," has a nice ring to it. I happen to like it a lot myself.

Held up to the mirror, it's beautiful.

About the Author

A native of Santa Barbara, CA, Jon Obermeyer is a graduate of Westmont College. He holds the M.F.A. in Creative Writing degree from UNC Greensboro.

Jon is the author of "The Reassurance of Ghosts" and "Salsipuedes" (poems), "The Winter Practice" and "Centripetal Force" (short stories), The Low Wire: Meditations on Loss and Creative Restoration" (essays), "It Happens That Fast," "Briarcliff" and "The Harbor" (memoir),"Myriad: A Poet's Guide to the Writing Life" and "Siren Call SF," a poetry-photography collaboration with San Francisco photographer Dwayne Newton (2019)

Jon was a finalist for the 2017 James Applewhite Poetry Prize. His poems have appeared in *North Carolina Literary Review, Northern Virginia Review, The Greensboro Review, Blue Pitcher, Tar River Poetry, the International Poetry Review, Edge of our World, Stroke Connections, Santa Barbara Magazine* and *Spectrum.*

Jon's short stories have appeared in *Equator, Cities & Roads, and O.Henry Festival Stories.* His story "Not Really Mine to Give" was runner-up in the 1982 *Santa Barbara News & Review* fiction contest. Clyde Edgerton selected Jon's short story "Confessions of a Pacifist" for publication in the N.C. Writers Network's Fiction Syndication Competition. His essays and book reviews have appeared in the *News & Record* and *The New York Times.*

He lives in Bethesda, NC near Durham.

www.ingramcontent.com/pod-product-compliance
Lightning Source LLC
Chambersburg PA
CBHW051830250726
48659CB00005B/1772